A RAGE TO NOSH

 By RUTH and BOB GROSSMAN

GALAHAD BOOKS · NEW YORK CITY

Library of Congress Catalog Card Number: 73-81656
ISBN 0-88365-083-5

Published by arrangement with Paul S. Eriksson
Designed by Arouni
Manufactured in the United States of America

To Dottie and Ida
Who Are Still Wondering
What Sins They Committed To
Deserve All This

PREFACE   If the American culture ever becomes extinct, it won't be due to the atom bomb; it will probably be because of overeating. We have become a nation of nibblers who dip their hands into cellophane bags of all kinds of greasy goodies which put fat on our middles, cavities on our uppers and burn in our hearts.

The art of *noshing* has been finely perfected through the ages by a long list of famous *noshers*. The first *nosh* of all time was the forbidden apple with which the serpent of the Garden of Eden tempted Eve. This must have been the first in a long series of low calory snacks: for in all the works of art depicting the first couple, whoever heard of a fat Adam and Eve?

Everyone remembers reading about those long afternoons when David played his lyric harp for King Solomon. But few people knew the good king was thinking about vitamins and nutrition when he uttered that famous line, "David, peel me a grape!"

Then there are the seeming eccentricities in *noshing* that, as time progresses, the next generations find difficult to appreciate. One particularly famous gourmet was Count Dracula who was on a liquid diet all his life, and then some. He had a passion for something that looked just like tomato juice; but it sure didn't taste like tomato juice. He was a vein man who left his trademark on all his guests—the family coat-of-arms: two holes on the neck.

Noshers have even been glorified in nursery rhymes. Everyone who has ever been read to as a child knows the story of Little Miss Muffet. However, it isn't too commonly known that she remained a "Miss" and had only spiders for friends because she was terribly overweight, although her mother claimed it was only baby fat. She would sit by herself on her tuffet all day eating the curds and whey which were part of the strict diet the family doctor prescribed.

Probably the most famous of all *noshers* was the portly King Henry VIII of England. His sumptuous dinners were the envy of all the citizens. They would last for hours and were as beautiful to behold as they were to devour. And between each course were served *noshes* of every size and description from the far corners of the globe. Henry, who had a particular passion for drumsticks (they say his mother made delicious chicken soup) had the nasty habit of throwing the bones over his shoulder with great gusto and excellent aim. He wasn't a neat eater, but he had a hearty appetite.

However, no one deserves more credit for encouraging hundreds of generations of *noshers* than the ubiquitous Jewish mother who is famous for her tons of stuffed cabbage, schools of gefullte fish and mountains of chopped liver. Lest she violate the Dietary Laws, she has seldom wandered from these traditional viands of the Kosher table prepared from century honed recipes. Our Grandma, who was a very traditional Jewish mother, has become a real *mayvin* of *haute cuisine* in the Kosher kitchen with her culinary contributions of Chinese, Italian and French cooking. Continuing in her own inimitable style, she has created appetizing *noshes* that "you don't find already at every *oys gehmatet* Bar Mitzvah and wedding reception."

We convinced Grandma it would be selfish to keep these unusual recipes to herself . . . and selfish, Grandma never was. So with gray hair neatly in place, a clean apron around her long vanished waistline and rimless spectacles mid-nose, she began to tell us how to prepare *noshes* "so delicious, the diet you can start tomorrow."

This slender volume has been gathered with the hope that it will inspire you to join the endless list of "*noshers* who cared." In this day of calorie counters and sugar substitutes, use this book with abandon and eat! eat! eat! It will probably widen the silhouette, but the true *nosher* learns to lower his eyes when passing the scales. For in his heart, he knows he's fat!

Brooklyn Heights, N.Y.   Ruth & Bob Grossman

TABLE OF ✸ CONTENTS

PREFACE   vii

NOSHES FOR THE PARTY,
SO THEY SHOULD DO
SOMETHING BESIDES
DRINK   2

Beef Mama Tung   8
Mrs. Dix's Mushroom and
    Artichoke Glop   6
Chicken Canapes of
    Mrs. Stein   11
Mrs. Antoinette's Cheesy
    Bread Rolls   5
Mrs. Livingston's Stuffed Eggs   13
Stuffed Tomatoes Henry VIII   7
Mrs. Jolson's Lox Biscuits   10
Picasso Party Mix   4
Bacon Frankfurters   12

SPREADS, DIPS AND
SHMEARS FOR CRACKERS
AND PIECES OF BREAD
THAT ARE TOO GOOD
TO THROW AWAY   14

Pate De Bergerac   16
Caviar Spread Khrushchev   20
Cheese Rolls Gauguin   18
Mrs. Quasimodo's Chicken
    Spread   19
Mrs. De Sade's Smashed
    Smoked Sable Shmear   22
Lox Shmear De Leon   26
Madame Lautrec's Spinach
    Spread   23
Mrs. Da Vinci's Ricotta Glop   25
Mrs. Goldwater's Green
    Party Dip   27

Mrs. Ranger's Avocado Dunk   24

NOSHES TO BREAK THE
DIET   28

Mama Tarzan's Tuna Toast   29
Mother Graham's Garlic
    Bread   36
Mama Freud's Bean Balls   31
Mrs. Leonard's Lox and
    Potato Knishes   32
Mama Hefner's Cucumber
    Cheese Canape   35
Mrs. Wilde's Saucy
    Artichokes   33
Mrs. Davis' Beets in
    Horseradish Sauce   34
Mrs. Whistler's Egg Mechiah   37
Stuffed Eggs Einstein   30

NOSHES TO PACK FOR
THE TRAIN   38

Mama Manville's Cheese
    Loaf   41
Mrs. Capulet's Antipasto
    Loaf   40
Chicken Eggs Mama Smith   42
Stuffed Eggs Mrs. Darwin   43

SALADS SO YOU
SHOULDN'T SPEND SO
MUCH TIME IN THE
KITCHEN ON A HOT DAY   44

Mrs. Hill's Herring Salad   48
Borscht Mold of Mrs. Pavlov   49
Mother Franklin Tuna
    Mold   46

Macaroni Marco Polo 47
Mrs. Rooney's Chick Pea
  Salad 50
Mrs. Adler's Chicken
  Walnut Salad 51

NOSHES SO YOUR GUESTS
SHOULD GO HOME
ALREADY, IT'S LATE 52
Mrs. Crater's Caraway
  Fondue 54
Mama Columbus' Tuna
  Canape 55
Mrs. Pasteur's Toasted
  Cheese Sandwiches 60
Mother Dracula's Omelet
  Toast 57
Bagel and Lox Von
  Beethoven 58
Mama Castro's Cheesy Bean
  Toast 59
Mama Tell's Rum Toast 53
Mama Durocher's Pizza
  Snacks 61
Mrs. Custer's Egg Nosh 62
Mother Boleyn's Egg Treat 56
Mrs. Arnold's Cinnamon Toast 63

. . . SO YOU SHOULD HAVE
A SWEET TASTE IN YOUR
MOUTH 64

Mama Medusa's Pineapple
  Mint Freeze 69
Mrs. Borden's Strawberry
  Mold 67
Mrs. Brando's Watermelon
  Mold 66

Mrs. Gleason's Frozen Punch 68
Mother Douglas' Marshmallow
  Ring 70
Mrs. Cranston's Rum Balls 71
Grapes De Madame
  Bonaparte 65

SOMETHING TO WASH
DOWN WITH 72
Mama Nation's Party Punch 75
Mrs. Turner's Rum Coffee
  Punch 78
Mama Stuyvesant's Cranberry
  Punch 77
Mrs. Jessel's Hot Punch 76
Mama Quixote's Wine
  Cooler 74

INDEX 79

A RAGE TO NOSH

NOSHES FOR THE PARTY, SO THEY SHOULD DO SOMETHING BESIDES DRINK

PICASSO PARTY MIX*

1–9 oz. package Rice Chex
1–9 oz. package Wheat Chex
1–10 oz. box stick pretzels
¾ lb. margarine
1 tablespoon garlic salt

1 tablespoon celery salt
½ teaspoon cayenne pepper
2 tablespoons Worcester-
shire Sauce

1 large can salted mixed nuts

Break the pretzels in half first and put together with the cereal in a nice big roasting pan. Now you can sprinkle all over the garlic and celery salt. Melt the margarine in a little pot and mix in the cayenne pepper and Worcestershire Sauce. Next you can pour this over the cereal and pretzels, put on the cover and you'll bake in a 250° oven for an hour. Every once in a while a little stir will be good. After the hour is up, take from the pan the cover and bake for ½ hour longer. Now throw in the nuts and mix up good. This will fill the house with such a nice smell, like popcorn at the movies. You can serve this warm—but usually, you'll put into empty jars from pickles or coffee or something and take them out when the folks "drop by." It'll make everybody thirsty, so with drinks you'll be generous.

* *MRS. PICASSO:* at her son Pablo's first exhibition looked around with amazement and exclaimed (much to Pablo's embarrassment), "For this I gave you art lessons? !"

4

MRS. ANTOINETTE'S
CHEESY BREAD ROLLS*

12 slices white bread, should be fresh
⅔ cup grated Cheddar cheese

Enough butter so you can butter both sides
Worcestershire Sauce for sprinkling

Butter first on both sides the slices bread. Then on one side each slice you'll sprinkle about 1 tablespoon cheese and a little Worcestershire Sauce. Roll up like a blintz each slice bread and stick in a toothpick, it shouldn't unroll. When you're finished sticking toothpicks, put the rolls under the broiler for a few minutes, you should get brown and a little crisp. Makes enough for 12 servings or maybe even 24 if you're a little stingy and cut in half.

* MRS. ANTOINETTE: used to tell her daughter Marie, "I still say you tease your hair too much!"

MRS. DIX'S MUSHROOM AND ARTICHOKE GLOP*

1 lb. mushrooms, chopped
  coarse
3 scallions, chopped
1 medium onion, chopped
½ lb. sweet butter
2–9 oz. cans artichoke hearts
  in brine

½ teaspoon thyme
1 tablespoon chopped
  parsley
1 teaspoon Gravy Master
2 tablespoons flour

Melt first the butter in a large pot and then you'll throw in the mushrooms, scallions and onion. Let this cook for 5 minutes and all the while you should stir. When everything is nice cooked, pour in the liquid from the cans artichoke hearts. Now chop up the artichoke hearts and you'll also throw them in. Mix in the thyme and parsley and then the Gravy Master and the whole thing you should let simmer for 20 minutes. When you're through simmering, mix the flour with a little water it should be smooth and not lumpy. Mix this into the pot and let it cook for a few minutes more so the mixture will get a little thick. When you're ready to serve, cut yourself up in slices a couple loaves French bread and let each one put a slice or two bread on his plate and then a few good spoonsful of the glop. This makes a nice hot hors-d'oeuvre for that big party you're going to have to take care of all those "obligations" you never asked for in the first place. Makes about 2 quarts of delicious glop.

* MRS. DIX: she used to warn her daughter, Dorothy: "Better you shouldn't mix in . . . what is it your business?"

STUFFED TOMATOES HENRY VIII*

36 cherry tomatoes
1 cup cooked chick peas
½ cup sesame tahini (sesame seed oil)
1 tablespoon lemon juice

1 clove garlic, minced
3 tablespoons water
Salt and pepper, so it should taste spicy

First, you should wash good the tomatoes and cut off from them the tops. These you'll save . . . don't throw away! With a little spoon or a fruit scooper, take out from the tomato the seeds. This throw away already! Who needs it? Now mix together everything else and push it through a sieve or spin in a blender until everything is nice and smooth, almost like cream cheese. Taste to see if a little more salt and pepper it needs. Now, if you have a pastry bag you can put this in. If you don't have the pleasure, so you'll make one. Fold up a nice big piece freezer paper into a cone and with a pair of scissors you can snip the tip. Fill it up with the mixture and you're ready. Into each tomato squish a little mixture from the bag or cone until it fills up. When you squished already into each tomato, put back the little tops you saved. This makes a nice nosh for a buffet table and everyone will think you've been catered!

* HENRY VIII: his mother steadfastly maintained, "It's only baby fat. . . . !"

BEEF MAMA TUNG*

3 lbs. nice tender steak, 1
inch thick
A pot hot oil
1½ cups water
2 packets vegetable bouillon
½ teaspoon Gravy Master
½ teaspoon powdered ginger

1 tablespoon soy sauce
Enough hot sauce to make
hot
2 tablespoons ketchup
2 tablespoons cornstarch in
¼ cup water
4 scallions, chopped

First you'll cut into 1 inch pieces, the steak. Now make good
and hot the pot oil and cook a handful meat at a time for
about 2 minutes each handful. Cook a little less if you like
rare, or a little more if you like well done. When each handful is cooked, (don't burn yourself! it's hot, the oil!), let it
drain good on paper towels and keep nice and warm in the
oven. Now the sauce we'll make! Heat up the water and mix

in first the bouillon. Throw in the ginger, Gravy Master, soy sauce, ketchup and hot sauce. Let this cook for a few minutes and then the cornstarch mixture you'll throw in. A little more you should let it cook until it gets nice and thick and then take off from the fire. Now the scallions you'll add. When you're ready to serve the sauce, you'll put it into a chafing dish to keep hot. The pieces meat you can spear with toothpicks and serve from the oven a little at a time so too cold they shouldn't get. With this dish you'll see you'd better serve plenty to drink. If your company is afraid "maybe it's too spicy," tell them they're right and let them eat pot cheese. With people like that, don't aggravate yourself.

* MAMA TUNG: mother of Mao Tse who used to qvetch to indifferent ears, "What do you want to fool with politics? Open better a nice restaurant!"

MRS. JOLSON'S LOX BISCUITS*

1–3 oz. package cream cheese   1 cup flour
½ lb. butter   ½ lb. lox

First, you should mix good together the cream cheese, butter and flour. When it's mixed good, in the refrigerator you'll chill for an hour. While you're chilling, chop up the lox so it's nice and fine. Now you can roll out the dough until it's thin like a letter from that good for nothing son at camp. With a 2 inch cookie cutter, cut into little circles. On each circle, put on a pinch lox and fold over like an envelope. Now you'll go into the oven and bake at 450° for 15 minutes. This makes 30 to 35 pieces, depending on how thin you rolled and how tight you pinched.

* MRS. JOLSON who, in an exasperated tone, was heard to tell her son Al, " 'Momma,' all right. But what is it with this 'Mammy'?"

CHICKEN CANAPES OF MRS. STEIN*

1–2½ lb. chicken
1 onion
1 nice fresh egg
1 teaspoon MSG
1 tablespoon soy sauce
1½ teaspoons salt

A nice dash hot sauce
1 tablespoon sherry
1 teaspoon powdered
   ginger
12 slices white bread
A pot hot oil

First you should bone the chicken. The bones you'll save for another time, a nice soup maybe. Now the pieces boneless chicken you should grind up in the grinder nice and fine. If it's not fine enough the first time, grind again. Also grind up with it the onion. Now you can mix in the egg, MSG, soy sauce, salt, hot sauce, sherry and ginger. Trim yourself from the bread all the crust and cut each slice into 3 pieces. Shmear on each piece some of the chicken mixture and fry a few pieces at a time in the hot oil until they get nice and brown. Drain all of these good on paper towels and serve hot. If you want, you can make these before you need them and in a hot oven you can heat them for a few minutes. You'll have 36 pieces to serve, if you don't steal one or two in the kitchen.

* MRS. STEIN: told her daughter, Gertrude, "I heard you the first time . . . why must you always repeat yourself?"

BACON FRANKFURTERS*

2 dozen little cocktail frankfurters	1 Kosher garlic pickle
	½ lb. sliced corned beef

First, cut a nice big slit in each frank and then the pickle you'll cut also into little pieces like matchsticks. Now put into each frankfurter a little stick pickle. When you've done that, each piece corned beef you should cut into slices about 2 inches long and maybe 1 inch wide. Exact you don't have to be! Now wrap around each pickle filled frank a little piece corned beef and stick in a toothpick it shouldn't unfold. Put the whole thing under the broiler for 10 or 12 minutes, the corned beef should become crisp. Serve nice and hot with maybe a little mustard. If you've got friends like we have who make *hazars* of themselves, you'd better double the recipe.

* MRS. BACON: mother of Sir Francis who prophetically warned her son, "Don't hang around with that Shakespeare boy. He'll do something and you'll get the blame!"

12

MRS. LIVINGSTONE'S STUFFED EGGS*

6 eggs, they should be hard-boiled
1 cup chopped liver

¼ cup mayonnaise
1 teaspoon paprika
1 teaspoon lemon juice

Cut first the eggs in half the long way and take out from them the yolks. These you'll save for later. Stuff good each half with a tablespoon chopped liver and arrange nice on a plate. Now on each egg you'll put one of the yolk halves and press it down a little, it shouldn't fall off. Mix up the mayonnaise together with the paprika and lemon juice and put on each egg a little spoonful. If you did everything careful and didn't drop an egg on the floor, you will have enough to give 6 people 2 pieces each. If you dropped and you're one short, don't take 2 for yourself, you probably noshed on the chopped liver in the kitchen all day anyway.

* MRS. LIVINGSTONE: told her son, the Doctor, "All right, so play in the woods already. But when you get lost, don't come crying to me!"

13

SPREADS, DIPS AND SHMEARS FOR CRACKERS AND PIECES OF BREAD THAT ARE TOO GOOD TO THROW AWAY

PATE DE BERGERAC*

1 lb. chicken livers
2 lbs. ground beef
1 chopped up onion
3 chopped pieces garlic
2 tablespoons chicken
  schmaltz
2 tablespoons vegetable
  shortening
2 fresh eggs
½ cup vermouth

1 tablespoon flour
½ teaspoon white pepper
½ teaspoon powdered ginger
2 teaspoons salt
1 teaspoon MSG
1 tablespoon chopped
  parsley
½ cup shelled pistachio nuts
½ cup pine nuts

Broil the liver for a few minutes first on each side. While you're broiling, you can also saute good the onion and garlic in the schmaltz and shortening. When the sauteing is all done, mix it together, *schmaltz* and all with the eggs, vermouth, flour and seasoning. Now, if you saved enough trading stamps and got a blender, put this, together with the liver, into it and blend. If you didn't save or you're old-fashioned, so then

16

chop everything up fine yourself. Now mix in the meat and nuts and the whole thing you'll put into a meat loaf pan. This pan you should cover with a little piece foil and into a bigger pan with about 1½ inches water you'll put it. Then, the whole *megillah* you should put into a 300° oven for 2 hours. The last 20 minutes take off from the pan the cover and let it finish cooking open. When you're all finished chill it nice and cold for at least 3 hours in the refrigerator. Now, when the company comes, loosen all around with a knife the edges and put the pan into a little hot water for a few seconds. Now, you'll turn upside down on a large platter and come out with a plop. Maybe shmear the whole thing with some mayonnaise, it should look pretty or sprinkle on a little parsley chopped.

* *PATE DE BERGERAC:* named in honor of the mother of Cyrano, who successfully admonished him, "You shouldn't alter Nature . . . besides, what's wrong with your nose?"

CHEESE ROLLS GAUGUIN*

¼ lb. Pimento Cheese, grated   2 cloves garlic, grated
½ lb. American Cheese, grated   1 medium onion, grated
5 ozs. cream cheese   A good pinch salt
           A little paprika

Mix up good everything except the paprika. Now you'll roll into 2 rolls about 1½ inch thick and roll these very nice in the paprika. Wrap yourself up in wax paper and into the refrigerator you'll chill for a good few hours. When you're ready to serve, slice up nice and thin and put on crackers. If you like, you can also decorate the top with a little olive or even a slice radish.

* MADAME GAUGUIN: she told her son, the artist, as he left for Tahiti, "Big shot! My son's too good for Fire Island!"

MRS. QUASIMODO'S
CHICKEN SPREAD*

2 cups diced cooked chicken	¼ teaspoon pepper
2 cups chopped ripe olives	2 tablespoons ketchup
1 teaspoon salt	4 tablespoons mayonnaise

1 teaspoon curry powder

Chop up nice the chicken, it should be fine. Now all the other stuff you can throw in and mix up good. In a refrigerator you'll put it and let it chill for a while. When you're ready to serve it'll shmear nice on strips of bread toasted. You can also decorate with a stuffed olive.

* MRS. QUASIMODO: mother of the famous janitor of Notre Dame who, when he was a child warned him, "If you keep making faces like that, your face will freeze!"

19

CAVIAR SPREAD KHRUSHCHEV*

1 slice white bread

3 tablespoons vinegar

3 cloves garlic

2 egg yolks

¼ teaspoon salt

1 tablespoon lemon juice

2 cups oil

3 tablespoons red caviar

8 oz. package cream cheese

3 tablespoons milk

Remove first the crust from the bread. Now break up good the bread into little pieces and let it soak in the vinegar. When it's nice and soft, in a towel you'll put it and squeeze until all the liquid goes out. Back in the bowl you'll put it. Mash up fine the garlic and add it also. Next, take a pestle and mash the garlic and bread together, they should make a fine paste. When it's nice and fine, throw in the egg yolks and salt and beat it good with a whisk. Add the oil drop by drop until it gets so thick it's hard to beat. Then it's O.K. to use the electric beater. In a small stream you'll add the oil while you're beating until it's all used up and the mixture is thick like old-fashioned sour cream. Then pour in a little lemon juice. Mash up the caviar, it should be smooth and then throw this in also. Soften the cream cheese with the milk and this too you can throw in a little at a time while you're beating. Until you're nice and smooth, you shouldn't stop beating. Then you can taste—if you need a little more salt, so throw it in. If a little more lemon juice, also throw in. Then in the refrigerator you'll chill until you're ready to serve with crackers, pieces pumpernickel or you can even spoon onto some avocadoes and serve for a fancy dish. Makes about 4 cups' worth and it's plenty rich!

* MRS. KHRUSHCHEV: Nikita's mother, who told him many years ago, "Shoes belong on the floor, not on the table!"

MRS. DE SADE'S
SMASHED SMOKED SABLE SHMEAR*

⅛ lb. smoked sable or other smoked fish
4 tablespoons sour cream
8 oz. package cream cheese
2 tablespoons chopped chives
¼ teaspoon salt
A good pinch pepper

Break up to a fine paste the smoked fish. Make sure the bones you'll take out so you shouldn't choke. Now mix it all up together with everything else and serve it with crackers so the family shouldn't starve when they're watching TV.

* MRS. DE SADE: mother of the famous Marquis, who constantly admonished her aggressive son, "Don't hit! Play nice!"

MADAME LAUTREC'S
SPINACH SPREAD*

2 packages frozen chopped
  spinach
4 cloves garlic

2 teaspoons salt
A good pinch pepper
1 cup yogurt

Cook the spinach together with the salt and enough water like it says on the package. When you're finished cooking you should let it drain and then chill it in the refrigerator. Next, you can chop fine the garlic and mix it in with the spinach. Sprinkle in the pepper and stir in the yogurt. Now let it chill good in the refrigerator until you're ready to serve. Put in on the table with little crackers or potato chips. The Mah-Jongg crowd will like this for a change. Onion dips and sour cream they can get at somebody else's house.

* *MADAME LAUTREC:* she warned her son, Toulouse, "If you don't eat your spinach, you'll never grow up!"

MRS. RANGER'S AVOCADO DUNK*

2 avocados, mashed-up
2 tomatoes, peeled and
   chopped
¼ cup mayonnaise
2 tablespoons lemon juice
1 small onion, chopped

¼ teaspoon chili powder
A good pinch salt
Another good pinch garlic
   salt
A little cayenne

Mix together smooth the avocados, tomatoes, mayonnaise and lemon juice. Then throw in everything else and stir it up good. Give a taste to see if there's enough seasoning and then serve with crackers or celery sticks. You should be careful and don't make this too long before you need it, because it'll turn dark like an old apple. Good it will be; it just won't look so nice.

* MRS. RANGER: asked her only son, The Lone . . . "Why don't you wash your face once in awhile? You look like you're wearing a mask."

24

MRS. DA VINCI'S RICOTTA GLOP*

2 cups ricotta (or creamy cottage cheese)
2 small cans caponata (Italian eggplant appetizer)
1 tablespoon horseradish
1 teaspoon salt

1 tablespoon Worcestershire Sauce
1 tablespoon lemon juice
1 clove garlic, crushed & chopped
A good pinch cayenne pepper

2 teaspoons Dijon mustard

Blend good together in a blender 1 can caponata, the horseradish, salt, lemon juice, Worcestershire Sauce, garlic, cayenne pepper and mustard. Now mix all this in together with the 2 cups ricotta and the other can caponata. Chill it good and serve it in a nice bowl with little slices of black bread or even pieces cauliflower or carrots. It's a good shmear and has plenty calcium, your teeth shouldn't fall out.

* MRS. DA VINCI: she told her son Lennie, "If you can't make up your mind what you want to be, maybe better you should go into your father's business."

LOX SHMEAR DE LEON*

⅛ lb. lox   4 tablespoons yogurt
        8 oz. package cream cheese

Smash up good the lox, it should be fine like a paste. Mix it all up together with the yogurt and cream cheese. This is nice to serve on matzoh because it'll give it a taste and the saltiness is good for you on hot days.

* *MRS. DE LEON:* Ponce's mother who lamented to her friends at the sisterhood meeting, "So what's the big attraction in Florida? A girl I could understand . . . but a fountain? !"

MRS. GOLDWATER'S
GREEN PARTY DIP*

1–17 oz. can green peas
1–3 oz. package cream cheese
½ cup yogurt
½ cup mayonnaise

1 small onion, chopped fine
1 clove garlic, also fine
A splash lemon juice
A little salt
A nice dash cayenne

First you drain the peas and then smash them good in the blender or through a sieve you'll push them. Now you can mix in already the remaining things and then put it in the refrigerator, it should chill. When you're ready, you can serve with potato chips, crackers or pieces carrots, or cauliflower to dip. The nice thing about this dip is that this way maybe the kids will eat their vegetables.

* MRS. GOLDWATER: "When I think what I sacrificed so you could go to Hebrew School."

NOSHES TO BREAK THE DIET

MAMA TARZAN'S TUNA TOAST*

8 slices white bread
1–7 oz. can tuna fish
¼ cup chopped onions
2 tablespoons sweet pickle
  relish
⅓ cup mayonnaise

1 teaspoon prepared
  mustard
¼ teaspoon salt
A pinch pepper
8 slices tomato
1 cup grated Swiss cheese

Toast first the bread. Now mix up together the tuna with the onion, relish, mayonnaise, mustard, salt and pepper. Each piece toast you'll spread with this mixture and then put on top each one a slice tomato. Now the whole thing sprinkle with the grated cheese and under the broiler you'll put for 3 or 4 minutes so the cheese can melt and bubble like maybe a young volcano. This will be enough for 8 people for a snack or 4 people for a feast.

* *MAMA TARZAN:* often told her son, "Stop banging on your chest and yelling! All the neighbors are talking!"

STUFFED EGGS EINSTEIN*

6 eggs, should be hard-boiled   2 tablespoons chopped
6 tablespoons butter   chives
2 tablespoons chopped parsley   2 tablespoons mayonnaise
            A few pinches salt for a taste
            A couple sprinkles hot sauce

Cut first in half the eggs and take out from them the yolks.
Now rub the yolks through a sieve and then smash it good
together with the butter. Next, you'll mix in nice the parsley,
chives, mayonnaise, salt and hot sauce and with this mixture
you should stuff full the whites. Now you can chill yourself
good in the refrigerator until you're ready to serve to fancy
company, like the rich cousins from Philadelphia—even if
they didn't feed you so hot last time you were there.

* MRS. EINSTEIN: Albert's mother who used to *noodge* her son,
"A genius you don't have to be . . . but what kind of grades are
these?"

MAMA FREUD'S BEAN BALLS*

1–1 lb. 4 oz. can white kidney beans (Cannellini)
1 slice white bread
1½ teaspoons salt
¼ teaspoon black pepper
½ cup flour
2 tablespoons sesame seeds
A pot oil

Drain first the can beans and grind up nice in a grinder together with the slice bread. Now mix in the salt, pepper and sesame seeds. When you're all mixed good, put in the flour and stir so you'll have a mixture a little thinner than dough and a little thicker than latke batter. Now make hot the oil and put in the mixture in little tablespoonsful. If the first tablespoonful doesn't hold together, add maybe a little more flour. When everything is right, you'll fry already a few tablespoons at a time until they're a nice golden tan. Drain on a few paper towels and sprinkle on a little salt. You'll have about 20 bean balls, you should serve nice and hot right away.

* MAMA FREUD: "Sigmund! Don't eat fried food . . . it'll give you nightmares!"

MRS. LEONARD'S LOX & POTATO KNISHES

2½ cups mashed potatoes
½ cup lox, chopped up
¾ cup fine chopped onions
½ teaspoon salt
4 tablespoons oil
¼ teaspoon pepper
1 cup sifted all-purpose flour
1 teaspoon baking powder
½ teaspoon sugar
1 teaspoon salt
2 tablespoons vegetable
shortening
1 beaten egg, should be
fresh
2 tablespoons water
Another beaten egg

Cook first the onion in the oil until you get a nice golden color. Then you can mix in together with the potatos, lox, salt and pepper and let the whole mish-mash cool. Meanwhile sift together the flour, salt, baking powder and sugar. Now cut in good the shortening so the flour looks a little crumbly. Mix in the one egg and the water and knead it good with the hands, so it's smooth. If it's a little too sticky, a little more flour you'll throw in. On a floured board with a rolling pin you'll roll to about ¼ inch thick. Then you can cut into circles with a 2½ inch cookie cutter. Each of these circles you'll roll out a little more so they should be 3½ inches. On each piece dough you'll put a couple tablespoons potato mixture and put up the edges, it should look like a rose. When you do all of them, put them in a pan and brush yourself all over with the other beaten egg. Put the whole thing into a 425° oven and let it cook for 25 minutes so they should get nice and brown. Makes about 10 or 11 pieces and heartburn you won't get!

* *MRS. LEONARD:* "Jackie, *that's* how you talk in a Bar Mitzvah speech?"

MRS. WILDE'S SAUCY ARTICHOKES*

6 artichokes
A little salt
1½ cups mayonnaise
3 cloves garlic, chopped

3 tablespoons onion,
   chopped fine
1 tablespoon lemon juice
1½ teaspoons celery salt

1 tablespoon soy sauce

Fix up first the artichokes. Wash them nice and cut off from them the stems and about ½ inch of the top. Trim off also the tough outside leaves. Now force open the inside of the artichoke and scoop out from it the hairy "choke." (It's called that because that's what you do if you eat it.) Now in a pot with an inch water and a little salt you'll put the artichokes. Put on tight the cover and let them steam for about a half hour. While you're steaming, you can make the sauce. Mix together all the other things from the mayonnaise to the soy sauce, and put it into the refrigerator so a little chill it should get. Now look at the artichokes. If a leaf you can pull out easy, it's done. Drain off from them the water and let them cool. When they get room temperature, you can serve. Each person should get an artichoke and a little dish sauce so he can dip the leaves. It's not a conventional dish to serve relatives, and when you clear the table after dinner, you'll have artichoke leaves everywhere.

* MRS. WILDE: once declared to her son Oscar, "Have you been playing with my lipstick again? I told your father you should have joined the Boy Scouts!"

MRS. DAVIS' BEETS
IN HORSERADISH SAUCE*

6 beets cooked
½ cup onion, chopped
1 tablespoon horseradish

1 cup sour cream
A little hot sauce
1 teaspoon lemon juice

Chop good the beets they should be coarse. Now you'll mix up everything else and stir in with the beets. Until you're ready to serve, you'll chill in the refrigerator. When you're finally ready, serve it on little plates with tasty crackers. You'll have enough for 8 to 10 people, they should enjoy themselves.

MRS. DAVIS: used to say to her son Sammy, "With all the nice kids in the neighborhood, *you* have to play with the *goyim.*"

MAMA HEFNER'S
CUCUMBER CHEESE CANAPE*

1-3 oz. package cream cheese   ½ teaspoon Maggi seasoning
½ 5 oz. jar processed garlic   2 large cucumbers
     cheese spread   30 round crackers
         1 tablespoon paprika

Mix good together the cream cheese, garlic cheese and Maggi
seasoning. Now the cucumbers you should peel and cut into
¼ inch slices and then take out from them the seeds in the
middle. Each slice you'll roll on the edge a little in the paprika
and then you'll lay it on a cracker. Put in the middle of each
slice a little spoonful cheese mixture and chill for a little
while, so you shouldn't serve warm. This makes 30 fancy
canapes to serve at cocktail parties and ritzy Bar Mitzvahs.

* *MAMA HEFNER:* told her son Hugo, "No! You can't subscribe
to National Geographic. It has pictures a young boy shouldn't
see!"

MOTHER GRAHAM'S GARLIC BREAD*

1 long Italian bread   ¼ cup chopped chives
½ cup butter   A good pinch oregano
2 cloves garlic, chopped nice   A little salt and pepper

Cut first slices in the bread almost to the bottom and about 1½ inches apart. Now you'll melt in a pot the butter together with everything else. When you're all melted, pour into each slice a little butter mixture and good you'll let it soak in. Put the bread into a 375° oven for 10 minutes to get good and hot and maybe a little brown. Makes enough for about 4 healthy eaters, who should live and be well.

* MOTHER GRAHAM: used to tell her daughter Sheilah, "If you spend all your time gossiping, you'll never make a living."

MRS. WHISTLER'S EGG MECHIAH*

2 small cans anchovies
1 dozen hard-boiled eggs, chopped
1 small chopped onion
2 teaspoons parsley, chopped

2 teaspoons Worcestershire Sauce
¾ cup mayonnaise
A few dashes hot sauce
A little salt

Chop up fine the anchovies and all the other stuff you'll mix together with it. If it's a little dry, add a few spoons more mayonnaise. In the refrigerator you'll let it chill and then serve on little toast fingers. Better you should have plenty to drink . . . salt free this isn't!

*MRS. WHISTLER: constantly complained to her son, the artist, "With my back, I'd be better off in a straight chair."

NOSHES TO PACK FOR THE TRAIN

MRS. CAPULET'S ANTIPASTO LOAF*

1 1–foot long Italian bread   A few pimentos
1 clove garlic   5 or 6 slices lox
1 nice tomato, sliced thin   1 tablespoon capers
1 little onion, also sliced thin   A little vinegar
A little olive oil

Split first the bread down the middle and with the garlic you'll rub it all over. Now on one piece of bread arrange nice like a florist the slices tomato, onion, pimentos, lox and capers. Sprinkle on the oil and vinegar how much you like and put on the top piece bread. Press this good for ½ hour with a heavy weight (2 steam irons for this is nice) and then into pieces you'll cut up and serve. Makes enough for 4 Jewish heroes.

* *MRS. CAPULET*: "Marriage has enough problems already. Better you should go with a nice Jewish boy. Besides, I don't care much for his family."

MAMA MANVILLE'S CHEESE LOAF*

5 nice eggs, should be fresh   1½ teaspoons salt
8 ozs. Gruyere cheese   1 cup flour
¼ lb. butter   A few good dashes hot
1½ cups milk   sauce
       1 tablespoon caraway seeds

Put the butter in a sauce pan and on top you'll pour in ¾ cup milk. On a low fire this should heat until the butter is melted and the milk almost boiling. Meanwhile, you should make a nice paste with the cup flour and the rest of the milk and the hot milk you'll pour over. Now the eggs you'll beat up and mix in slow. Put this back on a low fire and mix in the cheese, you should cut in small pieces. Keep stirring until everything is nice and smooth and the cheese is melted. Now throw in the salt, hot sauce and caraway seeds. Mix these in nice. Take a meat loaf shaped pan and shmear all over a little butter. Now pour in the mixture and the whole thing in the oven you should put at 400° for one half hour. When it comes out it should cool nice and then you can cut into slices so you can serve. It's a nice dish at parties, and not so bad as a nosh the day after.

* MAMA MANVILLE: "Tommy, don't you think it's already time you got married?"

CHICKEN EGGS MAMA SMITH*

8 eggs, should be hard-boiled
1 cup cooked ground up chicken
A little salt and pepper
A little hot sauce
1 tablespoon chopped parsley
¼ cup chopped scallions
3 tablespoons mayonnaise

Cut first the eggs in half the long way and from them you'll take out the yolks and put them away, they shouldn't get lost. Mix up good everything else and put about 1 tablespoon of the mish-mash into each yolk hole. Take a few yolks and through a sieve you'll push them. Now sprinkle each egg with a little sieved yolk, it should be colorful. The leftover yolks are nice to put in chicken soup for the children. This makes 16 eggs to serve and who cares about the cholesterol anyway!

* MAMA SMITH: said to her son John, "Pocahontas? What is that, a Sephardic name?"

STUFFED EGGS MRS. DARWIN*

6 hard-boiled eggs
¾ cup grated Cheddar cheese

6 tablespoons butter
1 tablespoon mayonnaise

Cut first in half the eggs and put on the side the whites. The yolks you should smash up and mix with the grated cheese together. Now cream in good the butter and then put in the mayonnaise. Stir everything up until a fine smooth paste you get. If you need, a little more mayonnaise you'll add. Fill up each half white with the mixture and in the refrigerator you should chill. This is a nice snack; but with all that butter and mayonnaise, you should be ashamed if you take seconds.

* MRS. DARWIN: "Evolution Smevolution! What's the Rabbi going to say?"

SALADS SO YOU SHOULDN'T
SPEND SO MUCH TIME IN THE
KITCHEN ON A HOT DAY

MOTHER FRANKLIN'S TUNA MOLD*

2–6½ oz. cans tuna fish	2 tablespoons chopped
2 hard-boiled eggs, chopped	scallions
up	2 tablespoons plain gelatin
¼ cup chopped green olives	½ cup cold water
¼ cup chopped sweet pickles	2 cups mayonnaise

A little cayenne pepper

Chop up good the tuna with the eggs, olives, pickles and scallions. Now soften a little the gelatin in the half cup water and then over hot water you'll melt it. Then you can already stir in the mayonnaise a little at a time. When you've done this, the fish mixture you can also mix in. Grease good a mold with a little salad oil and put the mixture in. Now go into the refrigerator and chill for 3 or 4 hours so it should be firm. When you're ready to serve, dip the mold into some hot water and then turn upside down on a plate, it should plop out. With this you'll have enough for 8 people, if you serve also a little lettuce.

* *MOTHER FRANKLIN:* "Benjamin, if I catch you playing in the rain again, I'll take away your kite!"

46

MACARONI MARCO POLO*

1 lb. elbow macaroni	½ cup diced garlic pickle
1 large onion, chopped	1 cup mayonnaise
½ cup diced pimento	1 teaspoon salt (you'll add
1 cup diced Cheddar cheese	more if you need)
¼ cup diced green olives	½ teaspoon pepper
2 tablespoons vinegar	

Cook first the macaroni like it says on the box and then let
it cool. Now mix in everything else. If you wash good the
hands, it's easier to mix (and nicer if anyone's watching).
Don't be afraid, just stick them in and mix up good. When
you're all through, you can even lick the fingers to see if the
salt is enough. Now chill in the refrigerator until you're ready
to serve. Serves 8 to 10. You'll have it for days—and everytime
you pass the refrigerator, you'll see you can't resist.

* *MARCO POLO'S MOTHER*: whenever Marco left on a business trip remarked, "Whatever you do, don't speak to strangers!"

MRS. HILL'S HERRING SALAD*

1–12 oz. jar herring filets
4 large apples, peeled and
cored
4 medium sweet pickles
2 garlic pickles

1–1 lb. jar pickled beets
¼ cup oil
¼ cup vinegar
Salt and pepper, how much
you like

½ cup heavy cream

Dice good the herring, apples, pickles and beets. Mix together
nice with the oil, vinegar, salt and pepper. Until you're ready
to serve you'll let this stand in the refrigerator. Then you can
pour on the cream, mix up and serve on a piece of lettuce.
Depending on how big a portion you serve, you should have
enough for 4 to 6 people. If you don't have enough, you
shouldn't be embarrassed. Serve a little pumpernickel. This
will fill up nice.

* *MRS. HILL:* Fanny's mother who said to her daughter every
Sunday morning, "Will you get up already? You can't spend your
whole life in bed!"

BORSCHT MOLD OF MRS. PAVLOV*

3–3 oz. packs vegetable salad
   gelatin
3 cups borscht (from the store)
1 cup yogurt
1½ cups diced beets (leftover from the jar)
1 cup water

Bring first to a boil the borscht and then mix in good the gelatin, it should dissolve. Let it cool a little and then throw in the water and also the yogurt. Now the pot that this is in you should put into a bigger pot, with ice it should be filled. Stir it up fast until it gets a little thick and then the diced beets you'll mix in. Now into a 6 cup mold you should pour this and let it set good in the refrigerator. When you're ready to serve, you'll take out from the refrigerator and put the mold into a little hot water. Then quick you'll turn upside down on a plate and you're ready to serve. The nice thing about this borscht is that it doesn't splash and make red stains all over.

* MRS. PAVLOV: Pavlov's mother who told her son, "If you get a dog, I know who'll end up taking care of him!"

MRS. ROONEY'S CHICK PEA SALAD*

1 can chick peas
1½ cups diced leftover steak
½ cup wine vinegar
¼ cup oil
A good pinch salt
A little pinch pepper

1 medium onion, chopped
¼ cup sliced pimento olives
½ cup diced pickled beets
1 tablespoon prepared
mustard
1 tablespoon chopped
parsley

Mix together nice all the ingredients and serve on lettuce leaves because they're good for the digestion. Makes enough for Saturday afternoon snacks for the whole family and all visiting *yentuhs*.

* MRS. ROONEY: Mickey's mother who always told him, "Buy it larger; you'll grow into it!"

MRS. ADLER'S CHICKEN WALNUT SALAD*

3 cups diced cooked chicken
¾ cup diced celery
¾ cup chopped walnuts
2 tomatoes, chopped

1 green pepper, chopped
1 teaspoon salt
a little sprinkle pepper
2 nice hard-boiled eggs,
    chopped

1 cup mayonnaise

Mix first together everything except the mayonnaise. When it's all mixed nice, put in the mayonnaise and then mix good together again. In the refrigerator you should chill for a little while and then serve on lettuce leaves it should look nice. Decorate if you like with a few slices red radishes. You'll have enough for 5 or 6 people and if there's some leftover, it's nice in a sandwich.

* MRS. ADLER: often told her daughter Polly, "It's not nice for a single girl to have her own apartment!"

NOSHES SO YOUR GUESTS SHOULD
GO HOME ALREADY, IT'S LATE

MAMA TELL'S RUM TOAST*

1 egg
1 cup Grade A milk
½ cup rum
3 tablespoons powdered sugar

2 teaspoons nutmeg
2 teaspoons cinnamon
8 slices stale white bread

A little oil in the pan for frying

Beat good the egg and the sugar and then you'll mix in the milk and rum. Take the slices bread and for ½ hour you should let them soak in the egg mixture. Now, each piece you'll put into the pan with hot oil and you'll fry until you're brown. When you're all fried, sprinkle on the nutmeg and sugar and serve with a little cream poured over. You'll have enough for 4 people and aren't you glad you saved that stale bread, it's a sin to waste!

* *MAMA TELL:* always told her son William, "Don't play with your food . . . eat it!"

MRS. CRATER'S CARAWAY FONDUE*

1 cup dry white wine	2 tablespoons flour
1½ cups grated American cheese	A good pinch salt
	1 teaspoon caraway seeds
1½ cups grated Swiss cheese	A loaf French bread

This is nice to serve at the table so in a chafing dish you should cook. If you haven't got a chafing dish, a pot is also O.K. Heat up first the wine to a good simmer. Mix together all the cheeses with the flour and salt and mix it into the hot wine. Cook it and stir good until the cheese is melted and the mish-mash is smooth. Now sprinkle in the caraway seeds and serve it with big chunks French bread. This should be enough for 3 or 4 people on a cold night after the movies or on a cold night after anything. Look, what you do in your house is your business.

* MRS. CRATER, the Judge's mother who warned him, "If you're not home by midnight, don't bother coming home at all!"

MAMA COLUMBUS' TUNA CANAPE*

½ cup ketchup
2 tablespoons mayonnaise
1 tablespoon chopped onion
4 strips anchovies, chopped or
  smashed
1 tablespoon chopped capers
2 tablespoons chopped
  pimentos

2 tablespoons chopped
  black olives
1 tablespoon Worcester-
  shire Sauce
1–7 oz. can tuna fish
  mashed in flakes
6 slices white bread

Make sure everything is chopped up nice and fine. Then all
of it you'll mix together with the mayonnaise, ketchup and
Worcestershire Sauce. Now trim off from the white bread
the crust. This you'll throw away. Shmear each piece bread
with plenty tuna mixture and then put them under the
broiler for 5 minutes so they'll get nice and hot. You'll have
enough for 6 people who'll lick their fingers and ask for more.

* *MAMA COLUMBUS:* asked her son, the sailor, "Those are
names for ships? What's the matter with the Lena, the Yentah
and the Tanta Rebecca?"

MOTHER BOLEYN'S EGG TREAT*

4 hard-boiled eggs
4 slices toast
1 cup ketchup
2 tablespoons Worcestershire
   Sauce
1 teaspoon vinegar

A little salt and pepper
1 tablespoon butter
1 teaspoon prepared
   mustard
A few dashes hot sauce, if
   you like

Scoop out first a little hole in the middle from each piece toast. Now in each hole you'll stand an egg. If you fall over, cut from each egg a little piece of the bottom. Now it'll stand! In a pot you'll put in the rest of the ingredients and so it's nice and warm, you should heat it. When it's already piping hot, pour some over each egg right away you'll serve it so it shouldn't get cold. There will be enough to serve 4 when out-of-town company suddenly pops in and needs a little fattening up!

* *MOTHER BOLEYN*: warned her daughter Anne, "Don't lose your head over him."

MOTHER DRACULA'S OMELET TOAST*

4 slices white bread
3 nice fresh eggs
2 cups grated Cheddar cheese

A sprinkle cayenne pepper
A little pinch salt
4 slices tomato

Beat good the eggs together with the cheese, cayenne and salt so you should get a smooth paste. Now butter all over the slices bread and into a greased baking pan you'll put them. Spoon the egg and cheese mish-mash onto each slice (divide evenly so everybody should be the same). Put on each a slice tomato. In a good hot broiler put the pieces for 8 minutes or so. They should be a nice golden color and shouldn't be runny. You'll have enough for 4 "skinnymarinks" or 2 "stout and healthy" kids (who don't need this kind of meal in the first place).

* MOTHER DRACULA: mother of the famous Count who constantly complained, "Everybody else's kids kiss their relatives; but not *my* kids. They have to be different!"

BAGEL AND LOX VON BEETHOVEN*

6 heavy (what else?) bagels   1–8 oz. package cream
1 cup black olives, chopped   cheese
½ lb. lox

First, mix good together the cream cheese with the chopped
olives. Now cut in half each bagel and shmear some of the
cream cheese on each one. Cover this up with a nice piece
lox and the whole thing you'll put under the broiler for 8 to
10 minutes it should get hot and a little crisp on the edges.
It makes, of course, 12 pieces you can serve the next time the
girls meet at your house.

* MRS. VON BEETHOVEN: Ludwig's mother who screamed
while Ludwig practiced his scales, "Why must you play so loud?
Do you think we're all deaf?"

MAMA CASTRO'S CHEESY BEAN TOAST*

6 slices white bread, toasted 6 large slices Bermuda onion
1–1 lb. can baked beans 6 slices cheddar cheese
A little Worcestershire Sauce A little Dijon mustard

Cover good each slice toast with the baked beans. Then sprinkle on a little Worcestershire Sauce and cover each piece with a slice onion and then a slice cheese. On each piece cheese you should shmear a little Dijon mustard and then under the broiler you'll put each piece the cheese should melt. You'll have enough for 6 people and it's nice to serve with this a little beer or chilled white wine.

* MAMA CASTRO: "Fidel, if I catch you playing with Daddy's razor again, I'll break your neck!"

MRS. PASTEUR'S
TOASTED CHEESE SANDWICHES*

FOR EACH SANDWICH YOU'LL NEED:

A little butter
2 slices American cheese
2 slives white bread

A few slices onion, sliced
like paper
3 strips anchovies

Butter good first the bread on both sides. Now you can put in between the slices cheese, onion and the anchovies. Put the sandwich under the broiler for a few minutes on each side until the cheese melts and the bread browns a little. This is a nice snack to serve with a glass beer to the men, they shouldn't get hungry watching football on the television.

MRS. PASTEUR: used to tell her son Louis, "I don't care what it looks like, you have to drink your milk!"

MAMA DUROCHER'S PIZZA SNACKS*

6 English muffins	1 teaspoon oregano
1 can tomato paste	4 tablespoons grated cheese
2 tablespoons olive oil	1 can anchovies, chopped
1 small onion, should be grated	nice

Mix together first the tomato paste, olive oil, onion, anchovies, oregano and cheese. Now you'll cut in half each English muffin and on each half you'll shmear some mixture. When you'll all shmeared already, put them under the broiler and you'll broil until you're nice and bubbly and the edges a little brown. Take out from the broiler and cut up into wedges. This makes a nice party treat and also your guests a little thirsty.

* MRS. DUROCHER: was often heard to say, "Leo, with a mouth like that you'll never hold a job!"

MRS. CUSTER'S EGG NOSH*

4 nice fresh eggs   1 can undiluted chicken
1 small can mushrooms   noodle soup

Beat up good first the eggs. Now throw in the mushrooms
and the soup and maybe a little pepper. Salt you'll get enough
from the soup. Put this into a pan with a little margarine and
scramble. When it's ready to serve, on hot toast you can
put it. This makes enough for 2 people who like midnight
snacks when the late show goes off—or even before.

* MRS. CUSTER: the General's mother who used to yell at him,
"Don't play with those kids! They're a bunch of wild Indians!"

MRS. ARNOLD'S CINNAMON TOAST*

½ cup sugar
3 tablespoons butter

1 teaspoon cinnamon
6 to 8 slices toast

Cream first together the sugar, butter and cinnamon. Now shmear it all over the slices bread. If you shmear thick, you'll have fewer slices than if you shmear thin. So take your choice. Now in a pan you'll put these and then into a 400° oven you'll go for about 10 minutes until the bread browns a little. Serve with plenty of coffee for a nice breakfast (but go easy on the cigarettes).

* *MRS. ARNOLD:* told her son Benedict, "A word to the wise . . . nobody likes a tattletale."

. . . SO YOU SHOULD HAVE A SWEET TASTE IN YOUR MOUTH

GRAPES DE MADAME BONAPARTE*

1 lb. white seedless grapes   2 cups brandy

This you should make better a few days before you need.
Wash good the grapes and break into small clusters. These
you'll put into a jar and pour over the brandy. It should be
enough to cover. Let them stand for a few days and then you
can serve. Make sure to drain first—then, if you want, drink
the brandy. After all . . . it's too good to throw away. And
besides, it's good for the heart.

* MADAME BONAPARTE: "Napoleon! If you wouldn't bite
your nails all the time, you wouldn't have to hide your hand like
that!"

MRS. BRANDO'S WATERMELON MOLD*

2½ cups watermelon, diced
  and seeded
2 cups water
½ cup orange juice

½ cup lemon juice
2½ cups sugar
¼ teaspoon mint extract

Put together in a pot the water, orange juice, lemon juice and sugar. Bring this to a nice boil and then you'll simmer for 5 minutes. Now let it cool and then throw in the mint extract. The whole thing you'll blend in a blender together with the diced watermelon and the juice left over from the dicing. When you're blended nice, pour it into a 2 quart mold and freeze for 4 hours. When you're ready to serve, dip yourself into a bowl hot water and then quick turn upside down on a plate. This will make enough for 8 people who need something cool on a hot day, they shouldn't get sunstroke.

* *MRS. BRANDO:* used to say to her son, Marlon, "Believe me, I'll bet Mrs. Stanislavsky wouldn't have let her son mumble and scratch the way you do either!"

MRS. BORDEN'S STRAWBERRY MOLD*

1½ cups hulled and washed strawberries
2 tablespoons sugar
2 cups boiling water
1 cup cold water
2–3 oz. packages strawberry gelatin
1 cup yogurt

Smash up good the strawberries with the sugar and let it stand until you're ready. Next, dissolve the gelatin in a bowl with the boiling water and then you'll pour in the cold water. Now you can put this bowl into a bigger bowl full with ice and let the mixture get nice and thick. When it looks like it's enough thick, you can pour in the yogurt and beat it up good so you'll get fluffy a little. While you're doing this, on the ice it should still be. After it fluffs up, add the smashed up strawberries. If you have to taste a little, you can. Don't worry . . . there's enough! Now into a 1½ quart mold you'll pour the whole thing and chill good in the refrigerator until it sets nice. When you're ready to serve, you should dip the mold into hot water almost to the top for a few seconds. Then you'll turn upside down on a plate and you're ready to serve 8 people on who a little hives will make a healthy color on their cheeks.

* *MRS. BORDEN:* a New England mother who used to admonish her daughter Lizzie with the now famous line, "You'll put me in an early grave!"

MRS. GLEASON'S FROZEN PUNCH*

4 cups water	¼ cup strong tea
2 cups sugar	¼ cup lemon juice
1 cup pineapple juice	½ cup rum

Cook first together the water and sugar for 5 minutes so everything should be dissolved. Then mix in the pineapple juice, tea and lemon juice. Now you'll freeze until it's a little mushy and then the rum you'll stir in. Put yourself back into the freezer and let it get good and firm. When it's ready, you'll serve it in tall glasses and you should have enough for at least 8 servings to your guests at the Luau.

MRS. GLEASON: used to complain to her son, Jackie: "All the children in India are starving and you never finish what's on your plate!"

MAMA MEDUSA'S
PINEAPPLE MINT FREEZE*

½ cup canned crushed pine-
    apple
½ teaspoon mint extract
½ cup water
½ cup sugar

A little green vegetable
    coloring
½ cup lemon juice
1 cup ginger ale

Put together the mint extract, water, sugar and green coloring in a pot and you'll simmer for about 10 minutes. Then you should throw in the lemon juice, pineapple and ginger ale. Now in a refrigerator tray you'll pour and into the freezer you'll freeze for a few hours, it should be like a stiff slush. This will make enough for 4 people and it's not fattening like ice cream!

* MAMA MEDUSA: "That by you is a permanent? I'd sue!"

MOTHER DOUGLAS' MARSHMALLOW RING*

1 lb. marshmallows
1 cup strong coffee
¼ teaspoon orange extract

1 cup cream, whipped good
½ cup chopped walnuts

Cut up the marshmallows they should be in little pieces and then melt them slowly together with the coffee and orange extract in a pot. Now you can already fold in the whipped cream and pour the whole thing into a ring mold to chill. When it's chilled good and set, dip it into hot water for a minute and on a large plate you'll turn it out and sprinkle all over yourself the nuts. Makes a nice nosh for 10 people with "sweet tooths."

* *MRS. DOUGLAS:* Kirk's mother, who used to tell him, "If you eat candy like that, you won't have a tooth left in your head!"

MRS. CRANSTON'S RUM BALLS*

1 cup crushed fine vanilla wafers	2 tablespoons cocoa
1 cup confectioner's sugar	2 tablespoons corn syrup
1½ cups pecans, should be chopped	¼ cup rum
	½ cup granulated sugar

Mix together the crumbs, confectioner's sugar, pecans and cocoa. Stir in good the corn syrup and the rum. Mix everything up and roll in your hands into little 1 inch balls. If they don't roll easily, add a little more rum. Next, you'll roll each ball in the granulated sugar and chill yourself good in the refrigerator. This will make about 36 balls which should keep for a long time but won't, because they will be eaten too fast.

* *MRS. CRANSTON:* said to her young son Lamont, "You're so thin, someday you'll disappear altogether."

SOMETHING TO WASH DOWN WITH

MAMA QUIXOTE'S WINE COOLER*

1 can frozen pineapple-
  grapefruit juice, undiluted

2 cups dry red wine
2½ cups club soda

The wine and frozen juice you should mix together until the juice melts. Now into 5 glasses you'll divide this. Put in plenty ice and ½ cup club soda or seltzer into each glass. This makes a cool drink for a hot summer afternoon so you shouldn't have to fill up on egg creams.

* *MAMA QUIXOTE:* always complained to her son, Donald: "All the time, it's Sancho this and Sancho that! Why don't you go out with a girl for a change?"

MAMA NATION'S PARTY PUNCH*

1 bottle light rum	½ large can pineapple juice
½ bottle dark rum	1 can frozen orange juice,
½ bottle vodka	undiluted
2 cups dry red wine	1 large bottle club soda . . .
3 tablespoons Grenadine	(all right . . . seltzer)
½ large can grapefruit juice	

A little red vegetable coloring

Mix good everything together and in the biggest bowl you have. you'll serve it. Don't taste too much when you're mixing or you won't be able to pour too good and maybe you'll pour it on the floor instead. This recipe makes 1½ gallons . . . enough to make *shikkers* from the entire family and even some of the neighbors.

* *MAMA NATION:* "Mad money—a hat pin—even a whistle, I can understand. But, Carrie, why a hatchet?"

MRS. JESSEL'S HOT PUNCH*

1 quart dry red wine	3 slices lemon
¼ lb. brown sugar	½ cup orange juice
2 stick cinnamon	1 cup raisins
6 cloves	1 cup almonds, unsalted

Mix good together everything and let it simmer in a pot for
½ hour. This is perfect for warming the bones on a nasty
day, you shouldn't get pneumonia! Just in case, you should
also wear a sweater!

* MRS. JESSEL: "Georgie, don't talk at the table. Eat! Eat!"

MAMA STUYVESANT'S
CRANBERRY PUNCH*

1 lb. can cranberry sauce.   1–12 oz. bottle Bitter Lemon
2½ cups water   Quinine Water
½ cup sugar   ¼ teaspoon almond extract
           ¼ teaspoon mint extract

Beat good with a beater the cranberry sauce and the water until it's nice and smooth. Heat it up a little on the fire and mix in the sugar, it should all dissolve. When it cools off, pour in the Bitter Lemon and the almond and mint extracts. When you're ready to serve, chill first the glasses and pour it in over plenty cracked ice. If we knew how big the glasses are, we'd be able to say how many you can serve. This way all we can say is you'll have about 6 cups worth which, on a hot day, isn't enough, so maybe you should double the recipe!

* *MAMA STUYVESANT:* "Peter, I'm telling you the city is no place to raise children. Better you should get a nice place on Long Island!"

MRS. TURNER'S RUM COFFEE PUNCH*

4 cups milk, should be	2 tablespoons sugar
Grade A	½ teaspoon orange extract
2 tablespoons instant coffee	¾ cup light rum

Mix good everything together and in the refrigerator you'll get nice and cold. When you're ready to serve, chill first the little glasses by dipping in water and putting for a little while in the freezer. Then put in some shaved ice in each glass and you'll pour in the punch. L'Chayim! And what could be healthier than a nice glass milk with a little flavoring?

* MRS. TURNER: "Lana, so what if it's a little tight? It's too good to throw away!"

INDEX

INDEX

INDEX

ARTICHOKE
Mrs. Dix's Mushroom and Artichoke Glop, 6
Mrs. Wilde's Saucy Artichokes, 33

AVOCADO
Mrs. Ranger's Avocado Dunk, 24

BEANS
Mama Freud's Bean Balls, 31

BEEF
Beef Mama Tung, 8

BEETS
Mrs. Davis' Beets in Horseradish Sauce, 34

BEVERAGES
Mama Stuyvesant's Cranberry Punch, 77
Mrs. Jessel's Hot Punch, 76
Mama Nation's Party Punch, 75
Mrs. Turner's Rum Coffee Punch, 78
Mama Quixote's Wine Cooler, 74

BREADS AND SANDWICHES
Mrs. Capulet's Antipasto Loaf, 40
Bagels and Lox Von Beethoven, 58
Mama Manville's Cheese Loaf, 41
Mama Castro's Cheesy Bean Toast, 59
Mrs. Antoinette's Cheesy Bread Rolls, 5
Mrs. Arnold's Cinnamon Toast, 63
Mrs. Custer's Egg Nosh, 62
Mother Boleyn's Egg Treat, 56
Mother Graham's Garlic Bread, 36
Mrs. Jolson's Lox Biscuits, 10
Mother Dracula's Omelet Toast, 57
Mama Durocher's Pizza Snacks, 61
Mama Tell's Rum Toast, 53
Mrs. Pasteur's Toasted Cheese Sandwiches, 60
Mama Tarzan's Tuna Toast, 29

CAVIAR
Caviar Spread Khrushchev, 20

CHEESE
Mrs. Crater's Caraway Fondue, 54
Cheese Rolls Gauguin, 18
Mama Manville's Cheese Loaf, 41
Mama Castro's Cheesy Bean Toast, 59
Mrs. Da Vinci's Ricotta Glop, 25
Mrs. Pasteur's Toasted Cheese Sandwiches, 60

CHICKEN
Chicken Canapes of Mrs. Stein, 11
Mrs. Quasimodo's Chicken Spread, 19
Mrs. Adler's Chicken Walnut Salad, 51

DESSERTS
Mrs. Gleason's Frozen Punch, 68
Grapes De Madame Bonaparte, 65
Mother Douglas' Marshmallow Ring, 70
Mama Medusa's Pineapple Mint Freeze, 69
Mrs. Cranston's Rum Balls, 71
Mrs. Borden's Strawberry Mold, 67
Mrs. Brando's Watermelon Mold, 66

EGGS
Mrs. Whistler's Egg Mechiah, 37
Mrs. Custer's Egg Treat, 62
Mother Boleyn's Egg Treat, 56
Stuffed Eggs Einstein, 30
Chicken Eggs Mama Smith, 42
Mother Dracula's Omelet Toast, 57
Stuffed Eggs Mrs. Darwin, 43

FRANKFURTERS
Bacon Frankfurters, 12

KNISHES
Mrs. Leonard's Lox and Potato Knishes, 32

LOX
Bagels and Lox Von Beethoven, 58
Mrs. Jolson's Lox Biscuits, 10
Lox Shmear De Leon, 26

MUSHROOMS
    Mrs. Dix's Mushrooms and Artichoke
        Glop, 6

PARTY MIX
    Picasso Party Mix, 4

SALADS
    Borscht Mold of Mrs. Pavlov, 49
    Mrs. Adler's Chicken Walnut Salad, 51
    Mrs. Rooney's Chick Pea Salad, 50
    Mrs. Hill's Herring Salad, 48
    Macaroni Marco Polo, 47
    Mother Franklin's Tuna Mold, 46

TUNA FISH
    Mama Columbus' Tuna Canape, 55

    Mother Franklin's Tuna Mold, 46
    Mama Tarzan's Tuna Toast, 29

SPREADS AND DUNKS
    Mrs. Ranger's Avocado Dunk, 24
    Caviar Spread Khrushchev, 20
    Mrs. Quasimodo's Chicken Spread, 19
    Mrs. Goldwater's Green Party Dip, 27
    Lox Shmear De Leon, 26
    Pate De Bergerac, 16
    Mrs. Da Vinci's Ricotta Glop, 25
    Mrs. De Sade's Smashed Smoked Sable
        Shmear, 22
    Madame Lautrec's Spinach Spread, 23

TOMATOES
    Stuffed Tomatoes Henry VIII, 7

80